Dr. Cortesha Cowan

Presents

Recognize, Understand, & Embrace the Call of God on Your Life through Purpose, Passion, & Planning in 20 Days!

Recognize, Understand, & Embrace the Call of God on Your Life through Purpose, Passion, & Planning in 20 Days!

Scripture references were taken from the Holy Bible, King James version public domain.

Dedication

I dedicate this literary work to my family: Mr. Adrian Cowan, my husband… and my children, JA'Aaron Cowan, Adrianna Cowan, and Cortez Cowan, each of you have been unwavering in your support, love, and encouragement. Thank you for always being right by my side!

Love,

Dr. Cortesha V. Cowan

Acknowledgment

There are countless people that deserve recognition and appreciation because of their graciousness and support of me and my endeavors. However, first and foremost, I must give thanks to the Source of all sources... God! He has been with me through this entire journey. I am eternally thankful that God chose to utilize me as a vessel for this work. I am forever indebted to *Him* for His unwavering love, continual grace, and everlasting mercy. With God's help, I will aid you [the readers] in finding your purpose, passion, and plan so you can help others as well.

Adrian, my husband, we had been together since 1995... thank you for being my eternal partner! During the good and not-so-good times, we have proven to be unbreakable. You are my superman [singing with my best "Monica" voice] I love you so much!

To my daughter, Adrianna it has been my personal pleasure watching you grow from a sweet precious toddler to the amazing beautiful woman you are now. I am so proud of you... I love you immeasurably.

JA'Aaron and Cortez, my sons...thank you for being my greatness. Both of you are the heartbeats in my life. I am amazed by who you are. I love you! To my stepson, Darian, you are a bright light and the world will one day see everything that your family sees in you. Thank you for sharing your world and life with me. I love you always.

To my mother, Terri and my sister Dionne, who had always been available to help and do anything I asked of them. I love you both of you infinitely.

In Loving Memory of Those Dear to My Heart

My grandmother Lillie Mae White, My grandfather Johnny White, My grandmother Johnnie Mae Sanders, My grandfather Tilmond B. Sanders Sr, My father-in-law Henry Clay Cowan, My brother-in-law Aaron Cowan, My auntie Sherri White, My auntie Stephanie Sanders, My auntie Gwendolyn R. Woodson. Finally, my favorite uncles… Terry McClellan is known as Terrymac, Johnny White Jr, and Uncle Billy, Uncle Craig Huggins. Rev James White, Jr. I miss and love you all so much.

Table of Contents

Introduction 7

Day 1: The Acknowledgement of Purpose 8

Day 2: God Has Equipped *You* for *Your* Purpose 11

Day 3: The Believer's Obligation 14

Day 4: Own *Your* Purpose 17

Day 5: God's Sovereign, Talk to Him 19

Day 6: The Acknowledgement of Passion 21

Day 7: How is *Passion* Discovered 23

Day 8: Activate *Your* Passion, Be Electrified.................. 25

Day 9: Great Leaders are Passionate Leaders 27

Day 10: Living versus Existing................................. 29

Day 11: Acknowledge the Need of a Plan.........................31

Day 12: Organize *Your* Plan................................... 33

Day 13: Management is Vital for the Plan 35

Day 14: Short-term Planning 37

Day 15: Long-term Planning 39

Day 16: Trust God's Provision, it's ALL Love 42

Day 17: After the Discovery, Keep God First 44

Day 18: Don't Be Weary in Well-Doing 46

Day 19: The Continual To-Do-List 48

Day 20: Divine Mandate: His Purpose, *Your* Passion 50

About the Author: Dr. Cortesha Cowan 53

Introduction

Understanding who we are and why we were placed here on this earth gives us an undeniable advantage.

Fortunately, God will allow our purpose to align with our passion and respectively the plan to accomplish our purpose will manifest. Although, the manifestation may not materialize in the most conventional manners, it will emerge *on purpose for a purpose.* Consequently, the three powerful P's: Purpose, Passion, and Planning will advertently allow us to live our best God-led life. Do not be dismayed… "God has equipped you with everything good for achieving *His* will, and may *He* work in us what is pleasing to *Him,*" [Hebrews 13:21].

Achieve:

1. **Purpose** - the action/response of determination to do or <u>achieve.</u>

2. **Passion** – a strong and controllable emotion that compels <u>action/achievement.</u>

3. **Plan** - detailed proposal/blueprint for doing or <u>achieving *something.*</u>

Day One (1):

The Acknowledgment of Purpose

*There will be 5 days for the Purpose Journey

"Fight the good fight of the faith. Take hold of the eternal life to which you were called when you made your good confession in the presence of many witnesses." [Timothy 6:12]

Recognizing and knowing *our* purpose leads *us* to *our* passion. I vividly remember the day I understood *my* purpose. I sat at my dining room table while I reviewed my homework for one of my college courses. I felt an unresolvable sadness because graduation was near and almost 15 of the young ladies who attended school with me, contemplated dropping out because of childcare issues. I pondered, "What can I do to help"? At that very moment my purpose *found* me… it manifested as a clear confirmation of *who* I had always *been*… a helper!

According to my mother, I have always walked in *my* purpose… even when I was younger. I constantly ensured that various things happened to individuals who needed help. As an adolescent, my nickname was *Tishamommy* because I loved to help others and possessed the nurturing-loving aura of a mother [Thus "Mothers Helping Mothers" – My Purpose].

When *we* [my purpose and I] found each other, our connection was inevitably challenging at times, and required

direction from God. When helping others, difficult decisions and challenges come with the territory. However, the acknowledgement and understanding of *my* purpose are priceless, and the expected hardships pale in comparison to the satisfaction I constantly experience.

I pray, by the end of this literary and purposeful journey that *you* will understand what *your* purpose is and how *you* can utilize it. God will download the information you need to find your true purpose; the very reason you were placed *here* - on this earth. Within the next 20 days, I will guide you through the process of achieving your purpose... whatever *it* is. Be prepared for real action and possible tears, as God reveals *your* purpose - receive it! *Your* time *is* now!

The fact that you are in this moment, reading this book, and seeking God for direction... proves your readiness. Let's GO! It is time to find *your* purpose, so *you* can take the next step in *your* life. Regardless of the circumstances that [will] come, *you* must persevere! God has called *you* and *your* purpose is waiting!

"Commit your way to the LORD; trust in Him and He will do this" [Psalms 37:5].

Reflections

1. What is *your* purpose?

_____
_____
_____
_____
_____
_____
_____
_____
_____
_____
_____
_____
_____

2. Have *you* tapped into the missing pieces of *your* life?

_____
_____
_____
_____
_____
_____
_____
_____
_____
_____
_____
_____
_____

Day Two (2):

God Has Equipped *You* for *Your* Purpose

When God started helping me materialize my purpose, there were several days that I felt like quitting. However, God, consistently showed up *for* me right one time. Having *a purpose* is great, but what happens when a trial or tribulation rears its intimidating head? Personally speaking, I carried out my purpose daily… and the devil stayed on me daily. Fortunately, I knew God's Grace was sufficient, especially for my purpose.

I recall one day when I felt I had *really* started helping our teen mothers. The trials seemingly came in every direction that I traveled! I felt as if, the more I helped… the more things went wrong in my life. **Know this:** while on this mission, you must be girded in the Armor of God, this is how God allows *you* to carry out *his* purpose for *your* life. Also understand, the devil STAYS ready on *his* mission… to kill, steal, and destroy *you* and *your* purpose daily.

You must stay ready and keep the anointing on your life clean, so you can always recognize God's voice and hear Him clearly. This may seem hard but when *your* purpose from God is prophetic *you* have must keep *your* anointing untainted.

"Cast all your anxiety on him because he cares for you"

[I Peter 5:7].

Finally, remain prayer-full [filled with prayer]; it is a necessity as your purpose/message is delivered to the world.

Rest assured, your blessings/purpose cannot be hindered by the devil… because the message that God gave you cannot be stopped.

"Wine is a mocker and beer a brawler; whoever is led astray by *them* is not wise" [Proverbs 20:1].

You're the *only* person that can carry out *your* purpose. Thus, you must take care of yourself! The most significant form of self-care is prayer and the Armor of God, we are in a war with Satan and we need spiritual help. God provides protection and our victory is already sustained!

Reflections

1. How will you carry out *your* purpose?

_____
_____
_____
_____
_____
_____
_____
_____
_____
_____
_____
_____
_____

2. Have you ever felt as if you're your purpose?

_____
_____
_____
_____
_____
_____
_____
_____
_____
_____
_____
_____
_____

Day Three (3):
The Believer's Obligation

We must do our part as believers because God has shown us our purpose for the mission we are on; adversity, uncertainty, and weariness are certain, *but God* is ALWAYS in control, trust Him!

"Cast all your anxiety on him because he cares for you" [1 Peter 57].

When I left my job at Children's Hospital because of my obligation to walk out my purpose...everything [seemingly] went haywire in my life. I was down for a while, I thought I would never fulfill my purpose *completely*. However, I had to fight what I felt. I knew better, and I possessed the power to believe. I would not allow self-doubt to overtake me. I fought *it* every day, I was a faithful believer and dreamer... I still am!

God proved to me that if I gave it all to Him, my purpose was unstoppable. I knew exactly where I needed to be, and where I needed to go... the war room. Praying and warfare became a part of my daily life. I realized I have the power to change *my* mind... depression, anxiety, and self-doubt had no right to try and take residence where *my purpose resided!* You must understand the necessity of refusing to remain in a dark place; you must pull yourself out.

As a leader, someone who is obligated to help others you [will] need someone to pour back into you. So, get a mentor! Find someone you trust, someone who cares about you and will have your best interest at heart.

"Let all bitterness, wrath, anger, and evil speaking be cast away from you, with all malice" [Ephesians 4:31].

Reflections

1. Why are you fighting to fulfill *your* purpose?

_____

_____

_____

_____

_____

_____

_____

_____

_____

_____

_____

_____

2. What is the "Believer's" part, in your words?

_____

_____

_____

_____

_____

_____

_____

_____

_____

_____

_____

_____

Day Four (4):

Own *Your* Purpose

"The Lord is near to the broken hearted and saves the crashes in spirit" [Psalm 34:18].

You are the source of engagement for *your* purpose!

Be involved and remain involved, start strong and finish strong I every time. *Your* purpose is the greatest catalyst of your success.

When I started with the homeless shelter as an extension of our organization, I felt as if I substantiated my purpose *even more*! I was there daily… I helped and maintained my involvement in every program. Don't allow anyone to tell you that you cannot *be* a "hands-on CEO or employer! If your purpose requires you to be hands on and *not* to just sit in an office – own your leadership, purposefully!

God knows *your* true purpose and believe me it will make you feel better! Owning *your* core purpose not only helps you, but it helps everyone around you! When you own *your* purpose, you will *be* the change you desire to see in the world! I decree and declare, no weapon formed against you shall prosper. The purpose of your life *is to be* great, and nothing can hinder *your* purpose! You *will* do the things that God has called you to do.

"Rise up, come to our help, and redeem us for the sake of your steadfast Love" [Psalms 44:26"].

Reflections

1. What does it mean to own *your* purpose?

_____
_____
_____
_____
_____
_____
_____
_____
_____
_____
_____
_____
_____

2. How do you maintain self-direction?

_____
_____
_____
_____
_____
_____
_____
_____
_____
_____
_____
_____
_____
_____

Day Five (5):

God is Sovereign, Talk to *Him*

"Trust in God at all times, your people pour out your heart before Him. God is a refuge for us" [Psalm 6 -2:8].

Once I knew the purpose and plan for my life, I was happier. I walked with my head held high, because I knew no matter what - God's plans for me and the calling on my life is substantiated in such a way that other people's lives will be touched!

The Father's greatest desire for us, is that we know Him and have a-well established relationship with Him. The best way to connect, pursue, and fulfill your purpose is to know God's word and talk to Him daily! He listens intently and intentionally! Remember, all you need to do is ask.

"I will deliver you out of the hand of the wicked and redeem you from the grasp of the ruthless" [Jeremiah 15:21].

Reflections

1. What is *God's* purpose for *your* life?

_____
_____
_____
_____
_____
_____
_____
_____
_____
_____
_____
_____
_____
_____

2. What is the best way to receive *your* plan & purpose from God?

_____
_____
_____
_____
_____
_____
_____
_____
_____
_____
_____
_____
_____
_____

Day Six (6):
The Acknowledgement of the Passion

"And we know that the works together for the good of those who love God to those who are called according to his purpose" [Romans 8:28].

Now, that you know the purpose of your life, let's evaluate how *your* passion fits into the equation. The passion I have for teen mothers and their children is the motivation that drives my progression. On the days I feel sick, tired, and at times weary... *my* passion remains unaffected. Thus, it's easy for me to keep moving.

I was not sure why I kept moving until I began speaking on various platforms regarding passion. Being passionate *can* take you to the next level. Your passion makes you become a great leader. The acknowledgment that you know your passion ignites a fire that no one can extinguish. You will be an unstoppable leader within your purpose when your passion is relentless!

"Before I formed you in the womb, I knew you"

[Jeremiah 1:5].

Reflections

1. What is *your* understanding of *passion?*

_____

_____

_____

_____

_____

_____

_____

_____

_____

_____

_____

_____

_____

2. How will the discovery of *your* passion propel you to *your* next level?

_____

_____

_____

_____

_____

_____

_____

_____

_____

_____

_____

_____

_____

Day Seven (7):

How Is *Passion* Discovered?

"Restore to me the joy of your salvation and uphold me"
[Psalms 51:2].

Initially, I did not convey a suitable amount of patience relative to my passion. Sometimes I jumped in front of *my* passion because I was so zealous about my work.

Often, I moved be too quick… fortunately, I recognized my passion early on.

Everyone does not identify their passion right away, and it is okay. The passionate zeal that I possess today is the passion I desire to see in others! You are called by God to be a catalyst for change… don't *be* invisible and complacent.

When you find *your* passion, you will find your place in this world and further understand what you *can* and *cannot* do; *why* you are here, and the process of moving forward [with God] will be easy! The purpose of this workshop is for *you* to understand the calling on your life!

Reflections

1. Why you... Why is it your time?

_____
_____
_____
_____
_____
_____
_____
_____
_____
_____
_____
_____
_____

2. What does the discovery of "*your passion*" look like?

_____
_____
_____
_____
_____
_____
_____
_____
_____
_____
_____
_____
_____
_____

Day Eight (8):

Activate *Your* Passion Be Electrified

I know you want to have *that* feeling, but the process does not work like *that*! You must act on your *passion* and *then* that feeling [the electric tangibility *of being the change*] will manifest. Moving on the call on your life kindles *your* passion and it births an unmatched feeling of contentment.

Every time I ventured to Haven of Hope, to meet a teen mom for the first time, I was so beyond elated! I felt so alive, and happy because I knew I was working within my passion… it invigorated me. Our passion is compared to the love God has for us. Start with *this* love… its unchanging, unconditional, and progressive; when you possess *this* love for what you do [*your purpose*], then as you continually walk in it *your* passion the contentment of true satisfaction will manifest repeatedly.

"Therefore, we do not lose heart. Though outwardly we are wasting away, inwardly we are renewed day by day" [Corinthians 4:16].

Reflections

1. How will you *ACT*ivate *your* passion?

_____
_____
_____
_____
_____
_____
_____
_____
_____
_____
_____
_____
_____
_____

2. How will *your* passion allow *you* to show God's love to the world?

_____
_____
_____
_____
_____
_____
_____
_____
_____
_____
_____
_____
_____
_____

Day Nine (9):

Great Leaders Are Passionate Leaders

"Commit your way to the Lord trust also in him and he shall bring it to pass" [Psalms 37:5].

My trust in God is mandatory, He met me where I was, and God guided me into leadership! When I committed my work to the Lord, I was catapulted directly into my *purposed* place [leadership]. I did not *just* operate as a CEO, but I spoke life into the women and young ladies I encountered daily. This is the reason why I stand here today.

God molded me into an authentic leader *utilizing* the passion that I had to help young mothers. Initially, I simplified my purpose and passion to just giving young girls a warm place to stay … *but God* purposed more! I love being a leader; and I feel even more amazing because I'm *touching* and *changing* the lives of adolescent girls and women daily.

This platform is God-ordained, I know this because it exceeds *my* capability and *my* initial plan [Ephesians 3:20]. I never imagine being an author, a bestseller, or even speaking on *my journey* today… but I knew there was something *more* because the power that resided in my voice that pushed others… caused a stirring that was beyond me, it was/is divine! They'd shockingly say, "Oh my, God talks to Cowan, I'm getting goosebumps! Everything you've said is spot-on, and I'm so happy you're helping me!" In turn, I felt the same elation because God chose me as a vessel to *do this work,* on purpose for purpose!

Reflections

1. What is *your* definition of leadership?

_____
_____
_____
_____
_____
_____
_____
_____
_____
_____
_____
_____
_____

2. Why is it necessary to be passionate about your role as a leader?

_____
_____
_____
_____
_____
_____
_____
_____
_____
_____
_____
_____
_____
_____

Day Ten (10):

Living versus Existing

"I have seen his ways and I will heal him I will also lead him and restore comfort to him into his mourners" [Isaiah 57:18].

Living in my passion *is* a testimony, I say this because I am alive, but without knowing our true passion we can be alive but *not living*! My journey of teaching and helping others has not only given me a sense of fulfillment, but my vibrancy is contagious and it rubs-off on the ladies that I encounter... they are inspired, motivated, and compelled to move beyond their circumstances and into *their* purpose! I am genuinely living *my* best life ever!

"Merry heart does good like medicine, but a broken spirit dries the bones" [Proverbs 17:22]

Reflections

1.

_____
_____
_____
_____
_____
_____
_____
_____
_____
_____
_____
_____
_____

2.

_____
_____
_____
_____
_____
_____
_____
_____
_____
_____
_____
_____
_____

Day Eleven (11):

Acknowledge the Need of a Plan

"Blessed is the man who trusts in the Lord, and whose help is the Lord Jeremiah" [17:7].

Give God your plans; allow Him to be part of the daily planning in your life. Planning is an organizational action that articulates what needs to be done within a specific time frame; it can be hourly, daily, weekly, monthly, or annually… just plan! Sometimes planning does not turn out the way it should. However, our trust in God is the reassurance that *everything* will work!

The things we face daily are not as hard as we perceive them. God is a part of our daily plans thus; they will surely work together! I clearly remember numerous times that things did not go the way I planned, but God allowed everything to go smoothly at the appointed time!

Say this aloud: "I trust God to lead me through the planning of *my* life! I know His will for my life will manifest. I will trust in the Lord with all my heart and I will not depend on *my* understanding" [Proverbs 35].

Reflections

1.

_____

_____

_____

_____

_____

_____

_____

_____

_____

_____

_____

_____

_____

2.

_____

_____

_____

_____

_____

_____

_____

_____

_____

_____

_____

_____

_____

Day Twelve (12):
Organize *Your* Plan

This was hard for me! I always had the worst situations occur every year, relative to my planning. I did not plan as much as I should, because I allowed my *passion* to prematurely guide me [this is over zealousness]. I thought it out in my head, but to organize it was very hard. I thank God for a great team, they are God-sent lifesavers!

This part of your purpose is very important, because plans can make or break you! Most people need to organize their planning early on. This is one of the best ways to organize your plans, if you're not a great planner [like me], find someone who is, and ask God to guide you in the hiring process of someone who is a thorough and strategic planner! Someone who helps you prioritize, by aiding you with *your* time management skills so you can effectively balance your life, without feeling burnt-out!

Reflections

1.

_____
_____
_____
_____
_____
_____
_____
_____
_____
_____
_____
_____
_____

2.

_____
_____
_____
_____
_____
_____
_____
_____
_____
_____
_____
_____
_____

Day Thirteen (13):

Management Is Vital for the Plan

"Merry heart doeth good like medicine, but a broken spirit drieth the bones"
[Proverbs 17:22].

Don't try to make your own my way, because God's plan is perfect and may be different than what you thought or perceived. Simply confess, "Lord, whatever you have for me, I will trust You." He has the right plan for your life.

Think about how we plan and how we should plan with a God, I am not saying our plans are not good, I am just emphasizing the importance of keeping an open mind… because the plan for your life as *you* see it may change.
I had planned to simply be the best Founder/CEO for my organization, I had no idea that the more I walked in my purpose that God would take me down this road. I didn't expect to conduct workshops, or to be considered *the voice* of an often-voiceless community [teen mothers], I did not know I'd write three journals, and be a contributing author of various books! I am tremendously thankful for the road He has blessed me to travel!

I encourage you to keep an open mind because you never know what God will throw in the mix for you! God's plans are not our plans, so we must remember to remain open-minded and *always* ready! I never imagined being able to pour into others what God has poured into me… it is an amazing reflection of God's love!

Reflections

1.

2.

Day Fourteen (14):

Short-term Planning

I *guess* I can say, I've always been *good* at short term planning, I look at deadlines daily. Consequently, short term planning is great for me. I chart out a path for my week and achieving them is a great feeling. However, I don't get upset if I miss one or two deadlines; it happens. Don't be too demanding of yourself!

Take time to establish short-term goals to address all the tasks you have for the week. Keep God in your planning because without Him you are off-track *anyway*! God has too much to say and show you, so make sure you are taking the time to *hear* HIM…

Utilize the next few sections to reflect *intently*:

Reflections

1.

_____

_____

_____

_____

_____

_____

_____

_____

_____

_____

_____

_____

2.

_____

_____

_____

_____

_____

_____

_____

_____

_____

_____

_____

_____

_____

Day Fifteen (15):
Long-Term Goals

This section is designated for reflective long-term planning… trust me it *is* a lot to consider. Take some time to dream. Give yourself a deadline. This *will* help keep you on track. Don't get upset if you don't meet *every* deadline.

Take out a calendar/planner and establish preliminary start dates and deadlines. Remember, God knows the plan of *your* life… so, in this portion of the book, DREAM literally, WRITE purposefully, and PLAN strategically while conversing *your* BOSS… God is listening, and He provides the BEST guidance!

Reflections

1.

2.

Day Sixteen (16):
Trust God's Provision, It's ALL Love
Reflections

1.

_____

_____

_____

_____

_____

_____

_____

_____

_____

_____

_____

_____

_____

_____

_____

_____

_____

_____

_____

_____

_____

_____

_____

_____

_____

_____

2.

Day Seventeen (17):

After the Discovery, KEEP God First

Reflections

1.

_____
_____
_____
_____
_____
_____
_____
_____
_____
_____
_____
_____
_____
_____
_____
_____
_____
_____
_____
_____
_____
_____
_____
_____
_____

2.

Day Eighteen (18):
Don't Be Weary in Well-Doing
Reflections

1.

_____
_____
_____
_____
_____
_____
_____
_____
_____
_____
_____
_____
_____
_____
_____
_____
_____
_____
_____
_____
_____
_____
_____
_____
_____
_____

2.

Day Nineteen (19):

The Continual-Ever Changing To-Do-List

Reflections

1. Make a list of what you need to do and how to get it done. Include dates.

_____
_____
_____
_____
_____
_____
_____
_____
_____
_____
_____
_____
_____
_____
_____
_____
_____
_____
_____
_____
_____
_____
_____
_____

2.

Day Twenty (20):

Divine Mandate: *His* Purpose, *Your* Passion... It is RELEVANT

Relevant -closely connected or appropriate to what is benign done or considered.

"A gift opens the way in ushers the giver into the presence of great"
[Proverbs 18:16]

Leadership is authoritative guidance. The best thing you can do is trust God with your life, knowing that His plans for our lives are great ... He allows our passion to align with our purpose... and overall the path is smooth!

Reflections

1.

2.

About the Author: Dr. Cortesha Cowan

Within the next 20 days, you *can* stay on track with this mission; if you allow God to work things out for you! Dr. Cortesha Cowan, is a certified professional life coach, Christian life coach, holds chaplaincy license, an evangelist license, and has now provided you a step-by-step plan to utilize the 3P's within *your* life… Purpose, Passion, and a Plan to accomplish God's vision for *your* life! Dr. Cowan has nearly a decade and a half of experience helping girls and women find their purpose and passion. God has ordained her for this work, It is her sincere hope that you have been enlightened, impacted, and retrospectively equipped to realize *your* purpose, utilize *your* passion, and develop *the* plan for *your* destiny!